Jonas Brothers in Co

Featuring Leave Before You Love Me *and* Me

Arranged by Michael Story

INSTRUMENTATION

1	Full Score
1	Flute
1	Oboe
1	1st B♭ Clarinet
1	2nd B♭ Clarinet
1	B♭ Bass Clarinet (Optional)
1	Bassoon
1	E♭ Alto Saxophone (Optional)
1	F Horn
1	1st B♭ Trumpet

1	2nd B♭ Trumpet
1	Trombone
1	Tuba
2	Bells
3	Percussion I
	(Hi-Hat Cymbals/Snare Drum, Bass Drum or Optional Drumset)
3	Percussion II
	(Tom-Toms [2], Tambourine/ Woodblock)

8	Violin I
8	Violin II
5	Violin III (Viola 𝄞)
5	Viola
5	Cello
5	String Bass

SUPPLEMENTAL PARTS
Available for download from www.alfred.com/supplemental

B♭ Tenor Saxophone
E♭ Baritone Saxophone

NOTES TO THE CONDUCTOR

Jonas Brothers in Concert features two hits from the talented siblings—"Leave Before You Love Me" (with Marshmello) and "Mercy" (from *Space Jam: A New Legacy*). Although it is scored for full orchestra, this arrangement is completely playable by string orchestra alone, or with any number of added winds or percussion.

You may need to adjust the dynamic levels so the cello melody starting in measure 4 can be adequately heard. The percussion 1 part can be played by two percussionists, or by one on a drumset. In percussion 2, the woodblock part beginning at measure 42 could also be played on either a cowbell or claves.

The accelerando starting in measure 35 is rather abrupt—make sure your students watch the conductor carefully.

I hope you and your ensemble enjoy *Jonas Brothers in Concert*!

smartmusic.

Power Your Teaching

NOTE FROM THE EDITOR

In orchestral music, there are many editorial markings that are open for interpretation. In an effort to maintain consistency and clarity you may find some of these markings in this piece. In general, markings for fingerings, bowing patterns, and other items will only be marked with their initial appearance. For a more detailed explanation of our editorial markings, please download the free PDF at www.alfred.com/stringeditorial.

X	**–**	**,**	(♭), (♯), (♮)	⊓ ⊓ *or* ∨ ∨
extended position	shift	bow lift/reset	high or low fingerings	hooked bowings

Jonas Brothers in Concert

Featuring Leave Before You Love Me *and* Mercy

FULL SCORE
Duration - 3:15

Arranged by Michael Story

49437S

49437S

"Mercy (*from* Space Jam: A New Legacy)"
Words and Music by Amy Wadge, Nick Jonas,
Paul Jonas, Jason Evigan, Jordan Johnson,
Mike Elizondo, Sean Douglas and Stefan Johnson

49437S